SOFTBALL

FOR FUN!

By Darcy Lockman

Content Adviser: Joe Gordon, Men's Softball Coach, New York City, New York
Reading Adviser: Frances J. Bonacci, Ed.D., Reading Specialist, Cambridge, Massachusetts

COMPASS POINT BOOKS

MINNEAPOLIS, MINNESOTA

Compass Point Books
3109 West 50th Street, #115
Minneapolis, MN 55410

Visit Compass Point Books on the Internet at www.compasspointbooks.com
or e-mail your request to custserv@compasspointbooks.com

Editors: Deb Berry and Aubrey Whitten/Bill SMITH STUDIO; and Shelly Lyons
Designer/Page Production: Geron Hoy, Kavita Ramchandran, Sinae Sohn, Marina Terletsk, and Brock Waldron/Bill SMITH STUDIO
Photo Researcher: Jacqueline Lissy Brustein, Scott Rosen, and Allison Smith/Bill SMITH STUDIO
Art Director: Jaime Martens
Creative Director: Keith Griffin
Editorial Director: Carol Jones
Managing Editor: Catherine Neitge

Library of Congress Cataloging-in-Publication Data
Lockman, Darcy, 1972-
  Softball for fun! / by Darcy Lockman.
     p. cm.—(Sports for fun!)
  Includes bibliographical references and index.
  ISBN 0-7565-1682-X (hard cover)
  1. Softball—Juvenile literature. I. Title. II. Series.
  GV881.L63 2006
  796.357'8—dc22   2005025219

Printed in the United States of America.

Table of Contents

Note: In this book, there are two kinds of vocabulary words. Softball Words to Know are words specific to softball. These are defined on page 46. Other Words To Know are helpful words that aren't related only to softball. These are defined on page 47.

Spring Is for Softball

Softball is the most popular sport that people play in the entire United States of America! About 56 million men, women, and children across the country will bat, run, and field in at least one game in any given year. Are you one of them?

Softball was invented in Chicago in 1887 when George Hancock, a reporter with the Chicago Board of Trade, saw a disappointed football fan throw a boxing glove at a supporter of the opposing team. The man attempted to hit the glove back with a stick, and Hancock decided they should play a game of "indoor baseball." Hancock's game eventually became the softball we know today.

Like baseball, softball is a team sport in which a pitcher throws a ball to a batter on the opposing team. The batter tries to hit the ball with a bat, get on base, and score a run. There are differences, though, between softball and baseball. A softball is larger and less dense than a baseball, and the playing field is usually smaller. Softball games are also shorter, lasting seven innings instead of nine. Finally, a softball must be pitched underhand. It must be released by the pitcher when his or her hand is below the hip and no further from the body than the elbow.

The Diamond

Like a baseball field, a softball field is called a diamond. The 60-square-foot (5.4 square meter) area within that diamond is called the infield, while the area outside of it is called the outfield. The infield is usually dirt, while the outfield is generally grassy.

The field is divided into fair and foul territory. Fair territory is the field between the first and third baselines. Foul territory is any part of the field outside of the first and third baselines. When a ball has been hit into fair territory, it's considered in play. If it is hit into foul territory, it is no longer in play.

Key areas on the field are the bases and home plate, where each batter begins his or her turn. If we pretend that home plate is at 6 o'clock, then first, second, and third bases are arranged counterclockwise at 3, 12, and 9 o'clock. The standard distance between bases is 60 feet (18 m). Look at the diagram to learn the names of the parts of the field.

left fielder

third base coach

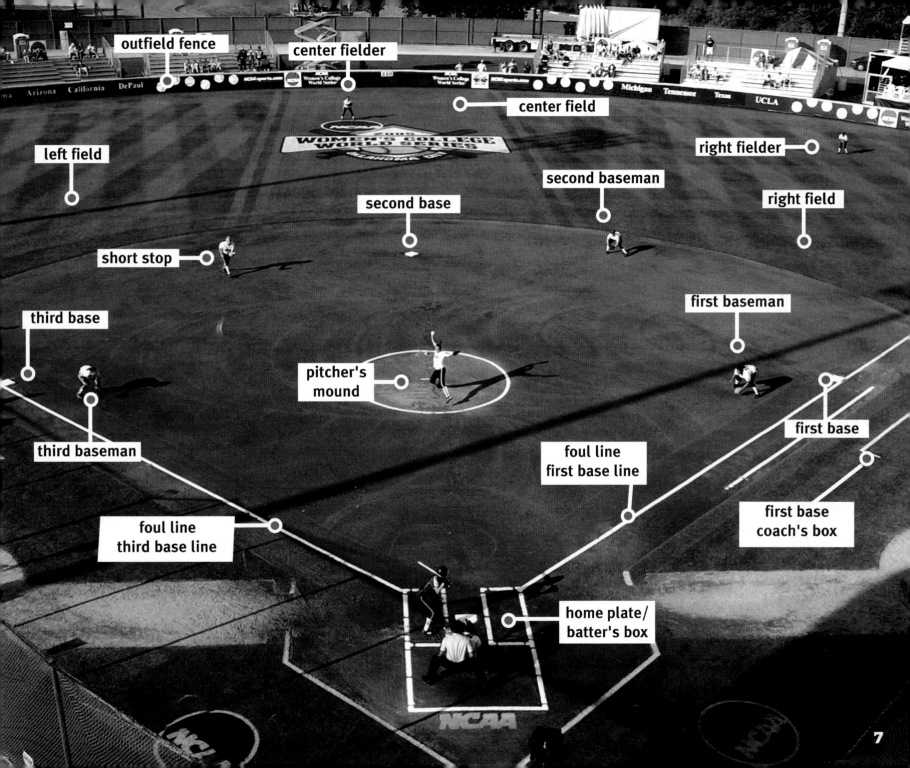

outfield fence

center fielder

center field

left field

right fielder

second baseman

right field

second base

short stop

first baseman

third base

pitcher's mound

first base

third baseman

foul line
first base line

foul line
third base line

first base
coach's box

home plate/
batter's box

7

The Roster

A softball infield is covered by a pitcher, catcher, first baseman, second baseman, third baseman, and shortstop. The infield players try to stop the ball and keep opposing runners from arriving safely on their bases.

There are two types of softball: fast-pitch and slow-pitch. Most slow-pitch teams use four outfielders; a left fielder, a right fielder, a left center fielder, and a right center fielder. Each uses the same players in the infield, but different ones in the outfield. Fast-pitch uses three outfielders; a left fielder, a right fielder, and a center fielder. Each of these players retrieves balls hit into the outfield.

Playing Just for Fun!

Sometimes softball is played just for fun and not for competition. Then the pitcher is a member of the batting team. This offensive pitcher tries to toss the ball in a way that makes it easy for his or her teammates to hit. In slow-pitch softball games with offensive pitchers, a rover, or short fielder, is added instead of the extra center fielder. This person plays between second base and the center fielder.

Hitting Balls and Touching Bases

In softball, the objectives of each team are to score runs and prevent the other team from scoring. The batting team has the chance to score. The fielding team tries to prevent the batting team from scoring. Each team has an equal number of turns at bat and in the field.

If your team is up to bat, players stand at home plate one at a time to try to hit the ball. When a batter hits the ball, he or she can run toward first base. If the runner arrives at first base before the fielders get the ball there, he or she is safe. When a batter hits the ball, the runners already on base can move to the next base. A run is scored each time a player touches each of the bases in order, making it all the way back to home plate. The team with the most runs at the end of the game wins!

Calling It Off

Softball games will often be called off at the end of the fifth inning if one team is beating another by a large number of runs, usually around 10. This is called the mercy rule, or the skunk rule. In the Olympics, play is ended after five innings if one team is beating another by seven runs.

Bats and Balls

The first piece of equipment you need, of course, is the softball itself. If you're just playing on a team for fun, you can dress informally. But if you're in a league, you'll probably wear a uniform. The other equipment you will need depends on what position you'll be playing.

An official softball for fast-pitch games is made of tree fiber or cork and rubber. It is about 11 inches (28 cm) in circumference and is covered with two pieces of yellow leather sewn together. A white ball may be used in slow-pitch games.

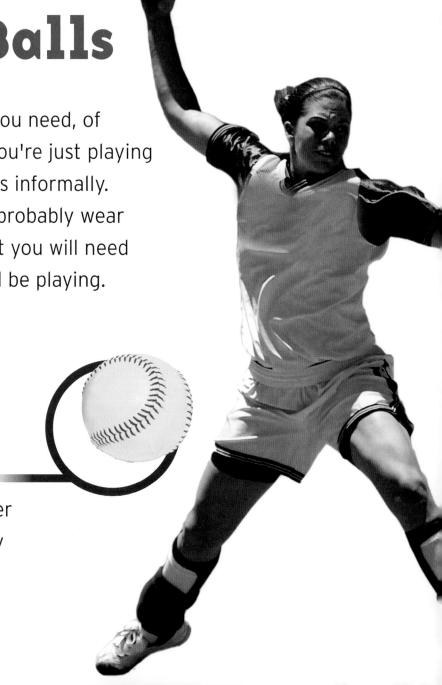

To hit the ball, players use a bat, usually made of aluminum. Lengths and weights vary, but bats can be up to 34 inches (86 cm) long and can weigh 38 ounces (1 kilogram).

The catcher and the first basemen wear mitts. A mitt has extra padding and no division between fingers. Other players wear gloves.

Softball batters usually wear helmets. Smart players always wear a helmet.

The catcher wears protective gear such as a face mask and a throat protector.

Play Ball!

Softball games are divided into seven innings. To begin play, the home team takes to the field while the visiting team goes up to bat. The pitcher throws the ball across home plate for the batter to hit. The batter can swing and hit, swing and miss, or not swing at all. Depending on the batter's actions over the course of multiple pitches, he or she will either get on base or be ruled out by the umpire.

The next batter will take his or her turn, and will also eventually either end up on base or out. The team's turn at bat ends when they have three outs. The teams then switch sides.

All About Innings

An inning consists of each team having one turn at bat and one turn in the field. It is the top of the inning when the visiting team is at bat. When the home team bats, it is the bottom of the inning.

Your Team at Bat

In a softball game, the team on offense is the batting team. The batting team sends one player at a time up to bat. The player stands on one side of the plate with a bat and tries to hit the ball that's been thrown by the pitcher. The player swings if he or she thinks the pitcher has thrown a good pitch. If the player hits the ball and it goes into fair territory, the batter runs toward first base. If the batter makes it to first base before the fielders get the ball there, it is called a base hit.

If the ball is hit far, the batter might make it all the way to second base, third base, or even back to home plate. Every batter's goal is to arrive at home plate in order to score a run.

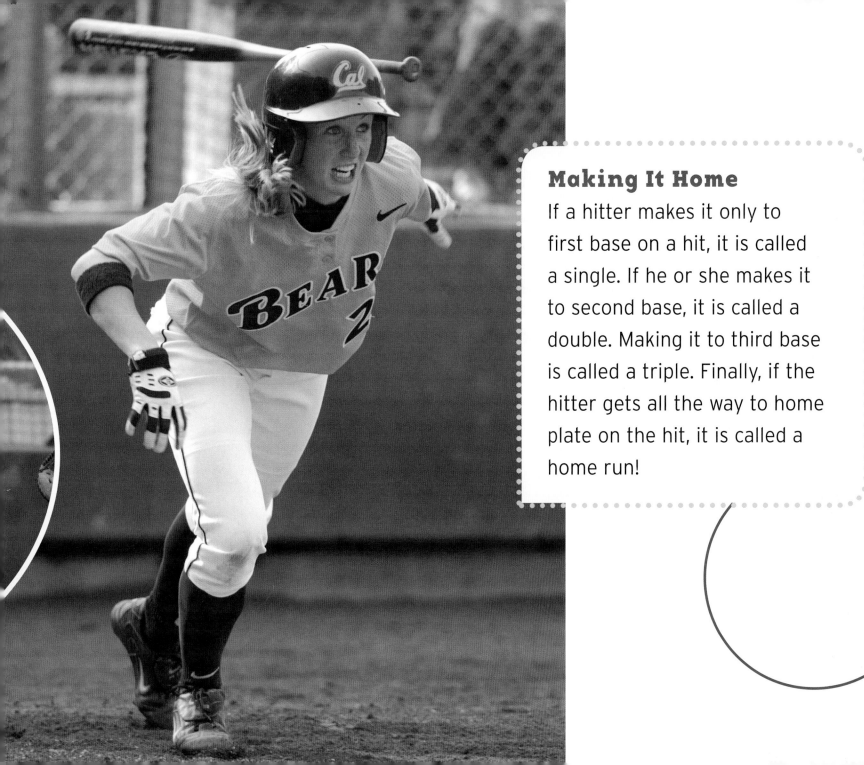

Making It Home

If a hitter makes it only to first base on a hit, it is called a single. If he or she makes it to second base, it is called a double. Making it to third base is called a triple. Finally, if the hitter gets all the way to home plate on the hit, it is called a home run!

Your Team in the Field

It's the fielding team's job to stop the batting team from scoring runs. Each defensive player has a different task. It is the catcher's job to receive the pitches thrown by the pitcher and to throw the ball back to the pitcher when the batter doesn't hit the ball.

It's the pitcher's goal to throw strikes. Strikes are pitches that cross the plate between the batter's armpits and knees and aren't hit by the batter.

When the batter hits the ball, it is the job of the fielders to go after it. If a fielder catches a ball before it hits the ground, the batter is out. A fielder can also get a batter out by stopping a ball that is on the ground and throwing the ball to the base the batter is running toward. If the ball gets to the baseman before the batter, he or she is out.

Once the fielders make three outs, half of the inning is over and the teams switch sides. Each team gets one turn at bat and one chance in the field per inning.

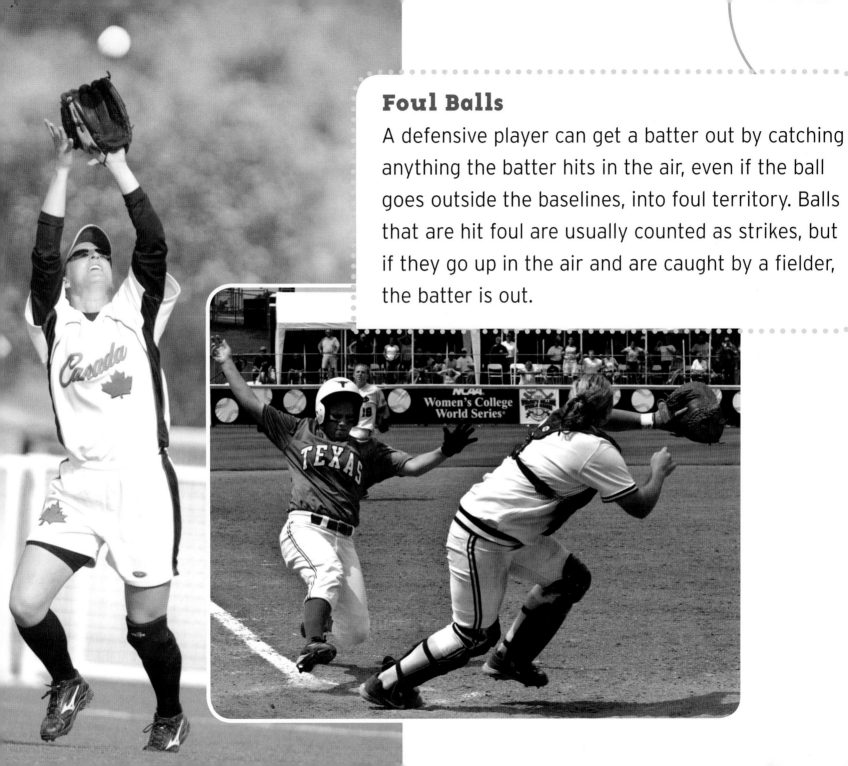

Foul Balls

A defensive player can get a batter out by catching anything the batter hits in the air, even if the ball goes outside the baselines, into foul territory. Balls that are hit foul are usually counted as strikes, but if they go up in the air and are caught by a fielder, the batter is out.

Batter Up!

Batters hit either left- or right-handed. Right-handed hitters are most common. They stand on the side of the plate with the left side of the body facing the field. Batters bend their knees while their bodies face home plate. They hold the bat behind their heads, with bent elbows.

A batter has two choices when receiving a pitch: to swing or not to swing. If a batter swings and hits, he or she runs toward first base. If a batter does not swing, the umpire decides whether the pitch was a ball or a strike. A strike crosses the plate between the batter's knees and armpits. This area is known as the strike zone. A ball is a pitch that does not cross the plate within the strike zone. If a batter swings and misses, this is also a strike. The number of balls and strikes for a turn at bat is the count.

The number of balls is always called first. Once a batter has four balls, he or she walks, or moves to first base without having to hit the ball. If a batter reaches three strikes, he or she is called out. Balls that are hit and land in foul territory are called foul balls. Foul balls count as strikes unless there are already two strikes in the count. In this case, foul balls are simply not counted at all.

Did You Know?

A batter who can bat both right- and left-handed is called a switch-hitter.

21

Leading Off, Tagging Up, Heading Home

A player on base is called a runner. A runner's goal is to advance from base to base without getting tagged out. Eventually, every runner wants to arrive at home plate to score a run for the team. To do this, runners have to move counterclockwise around the field touching all four bases in order, from first to second to third to home plate. Runners can move to the next base when a ball has been hit or when a hitter has been walked.

There are times when a runner is forced to run, and other times when a runner can choose whether or not he or she wants to move to the next base. Runners are forced to run when there is another runner who needs the base. Runners may choose to stay put when there is no one on the base behind them and if it seems likely that they would become out if they ran to the next base.

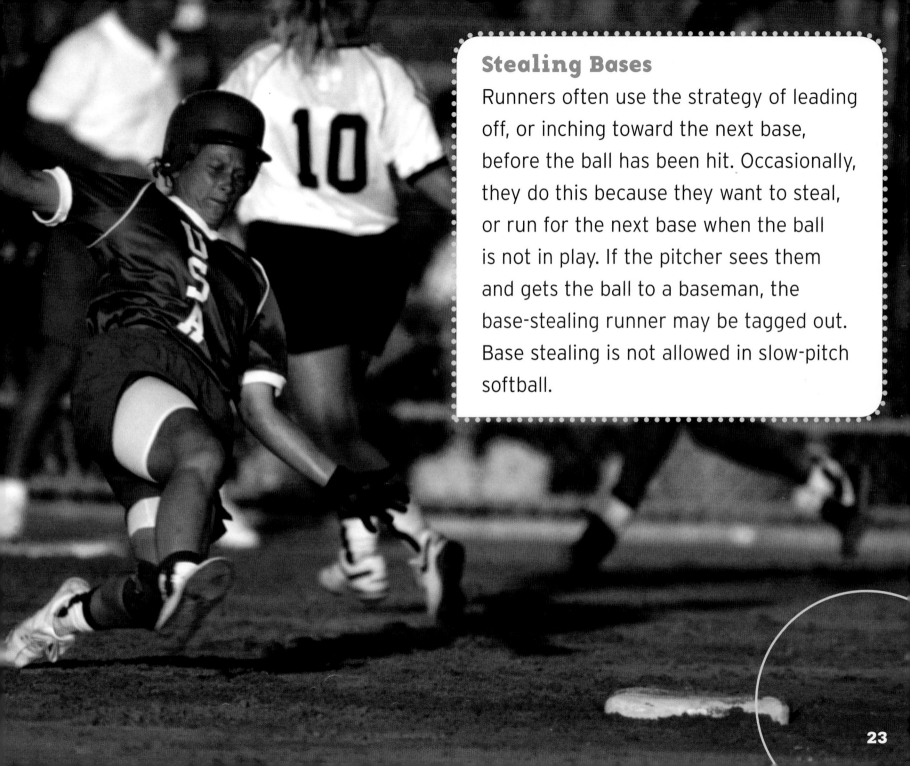

Stealing Bases

Runners often use the strategy of leading off, or inching toward the next base, before the ball has been hit. Occasionally, they do this because they want to steal, or run for the next base when the ball is not in play. If the pitcher sees them and gets the ball to a baseman, the base-stealing runner may be tagged out. Base stealing is not allowed in slow-pitch softball.

You're Out!

Batters and runners can either be safe or out. A runner is safe when he or she reaches a base before a fielder has tagged that base or the runner with the ball. A batter or runner can be out in several different ways. A batter can strike out by getting three strikes. A batter can also hit a fly ball. If the ball is caught before hitting the ground, the batter is out.

Once a ball is in play, runners can be forced to run. The fielder with the ball can make a forced out simply by tagging the base the runner is headed toward. If the runner is not being forced, it is not enough for the baseman to touch the base. Instead, he or she must tag the runner with the ball.

Tag Up or Get Out!

Runners can get ruled out when advancing on fly balls. If the ball is caught, the runner must tag up (touch the base after the ball has been caught) before moving to the next base. A runner who does not tag up on a caught fly ball will be out if he or she cannot make it back to the original base before the fielder gets the ball there.

Fast-Pitch or Slow-Pitch

The pitcher's job is to deliver the ball from the pitching mound to home plate where batters can attempt to hit it. Pitchers work very hard to develop both the mechanics and speed necessary to throw strikes. They often learn to throw different types of pitches that make it especially difficult for a batter to guess how the pitch will come across the plate. Once the ball has been hit, a pitcher becomes a fielder, just like everybody else on defense. Pitchers can make outs by catching line drives and fly balls. They can also assist in making outs by throwing balls that have been hit to the basemen or the catcher.

Pitchers use different throws for the two kinds of softball. In fast-pitch the ball is delivered to the batter at high speed with a flat arc, while in slow-pitch the ball is delivered more slowly with a higher arc.

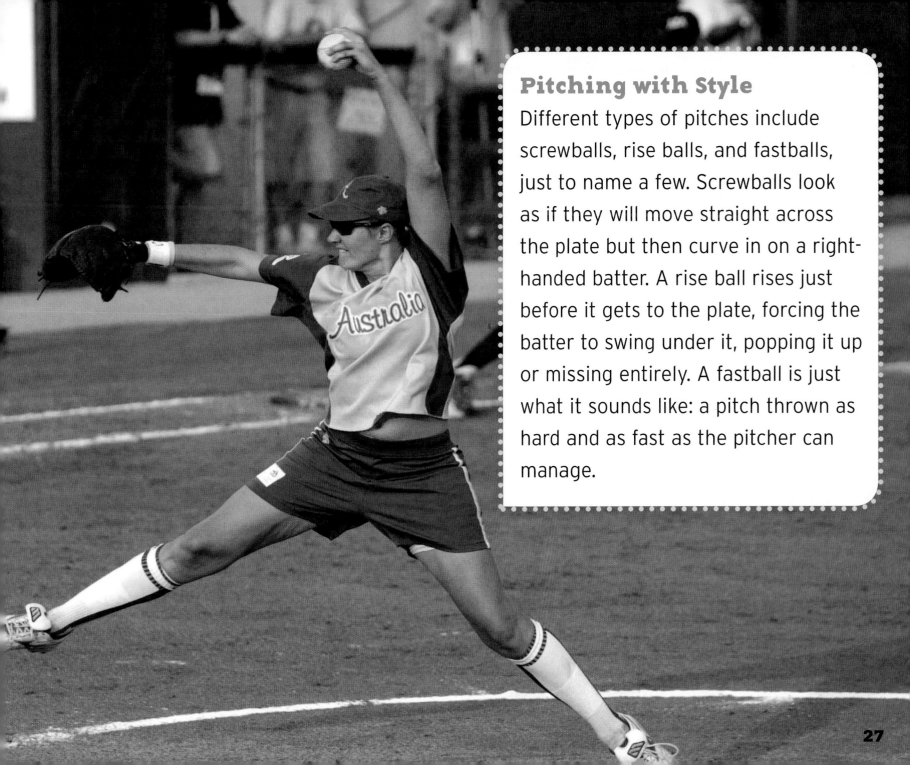

Pitching with Style

Different types of pitches include screwballs, rise balls, and fastballs, just to name a few. Screwballs look as if they will move straight across the plate but then curve in on a right-handed batter. A rise ball rises just before it gets to the plate, forcing the batter to swing under it, popping it up or missing entirely. A fastball is just what it sounds like: a pitch thrown as hard and as fast as the pitcher can manage.

The Person Behind the Mask

The catcher in a softball game can usually be found crouching behind home plate awaiting the pitcher's throw. However, the catcher's job is actually much more important than that. Because the catcher has the best view of the entire field, he or she is in the ideal position to direct the other players in a play. Catchers also communicate with the pitcher with hand signals in order to suggest pitches. To do this well, the catcher must be familiar with the strengths and weaknesses of both the batter and the pitcher.

Though the pitcher doesn't always follow the catcher's advice, he or she lets the catcher know what pitch will be thrown by signaling back. Catchers also hustle to catch pop flies and foul balls. Also, the catcher is generally the only fielder available to tag runners out at home plate, preventing the opposing team from scoring runs.

Danger on the Field!

The catcher's location on the field is the most dangerous position in softball. A catcher's game can be cut short by carelessly tossed bats, foul balls, wild pitches, and collisions with runners at the plate. For these reasons, catchers wear special protective gear on the field.

Calling the Game

Coaches make the most decisions about a team's play. The lineup, or batting order, is a choice that coaches make carefully. They often put their stronger hitters toward the front of the lineup. Coaches must also decide who plays each position on the field. Finally, two coaches are often in the field when their team is at bat to instruct the runners whether to run or to stick after a ball has been hit.

Umpires make decisions about pitches and outs. There may be anywhere from one to seven umpires in a game. The plate umpire stands at home plate and decides whether the pitches are balls or strikes. There can be up to three base umpires, and their job is to decide whether runners are safe or out. This can be a tricky call when runners arrive on base just as the basemen are tagging it.

Finally, there can be up to three umpires stationed in the outfield, where they will need to determine whether balls are hit into fair or foul territory.

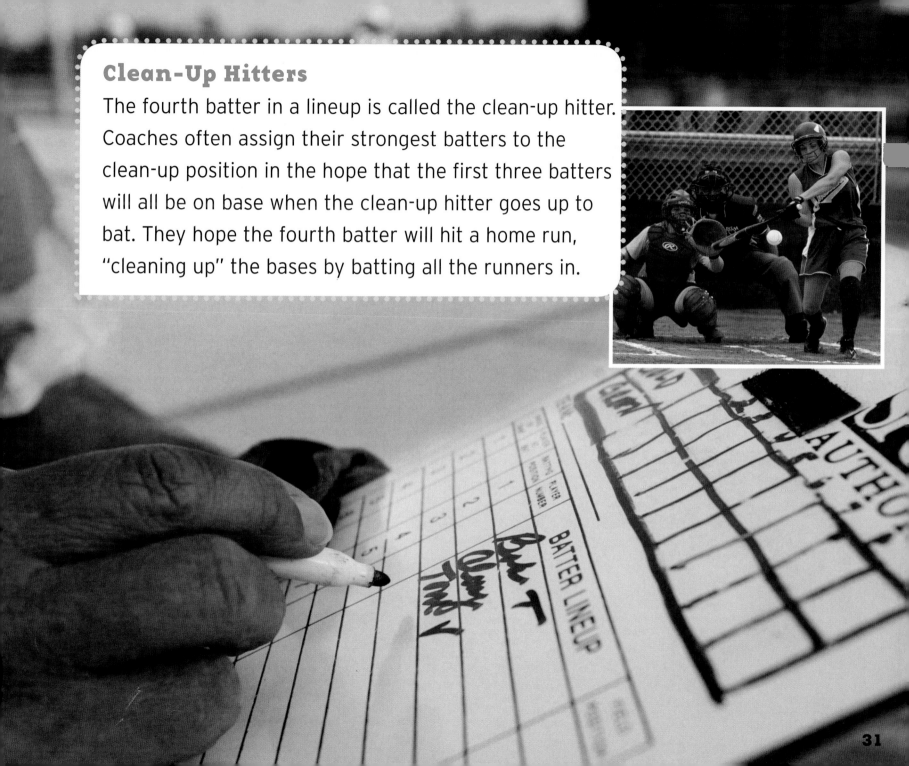

Clean-Up Hitters

The fourth batter in a lineup is called the clean-up hitter. Coaches often assign their strongest batters to the clean-up position in the hope that the first three batters will all be on base when the clean-up hitter goes up to bat. They hope the fourth batter will hit a home run, "cleaning up" the bases by batting all the runners in.

Offensive and Defensive

In softball, as in other team sports, it is common to use both offensive and defensive strategies. Offensive strategies are used to get runners to home plate when there are fewer than two outs, usually by sacrificing the hitter. Squeeze plays, sacrifice fly balls, and bunts (which are only legal in fast-pitch softball) may allow a runner to advance a base as the hitter is getting called out.

Defensive strategies are chosen depending on the placement of runners on base. For example, if a coach wants the team to be able to force an out, he or she may instruct the pitcher to walk a hitter in order to load the bases. The strategy chosen by a coach depends upon many things, including the specific talents and limitations of the players, as well as the score of the game.

A Legacy of Leagues

There are thousands of local softball leagues across the United States. Americans play informally after school or work and also in organized leagues through schools, parks, and recreation centers nationwide.

The official governing body of softball in the United States is the Amateur Softball Association. Founded in 1933, it standardized softball so that the rules are the same no matter where the game is being played. Official ASA teams have the opportunity to participate in tournaments and even national championships. Many players who have gone on to play in the Olympics and the Pan American Games came to national attention through ASA tournament play. It is one of the largest sports organizations in the country, with more than 250,000 teams registered.

Women in the United States also have the chance to play competitive softball both at the college level and professionally. The National Collegiate Athletic Association (NCAA) awarded its first women's softball championship in 1982. The NCAA women's softball championship series has become known as the Women's College World Series.

Let's Hear It for the Girls!

The first professional softball league for women was organized in the 1970s by professional female athletes from several other sports. This league lasted only four seasons. The idea for professional women's softball was revived in the late 1990s, and today National Pro Fastpitch has six teams that participate in 144 games a season.

The Big Wide World of Softball

Though softball was first played in the United States and remains most popular in this country, it is also played competitively internationally. The International Softball Foundation was founded in 1951 to standardize rules around the world. Today the foundation, which has its headquarters in Florida, even holds world championship tournaments in different categories every four years. Softball is also an official sport of the Pan American Games. The Pan American Games are like a mini Olympics, where teams from North, South, and Central America, as well as the Caribbean, are invited to play.

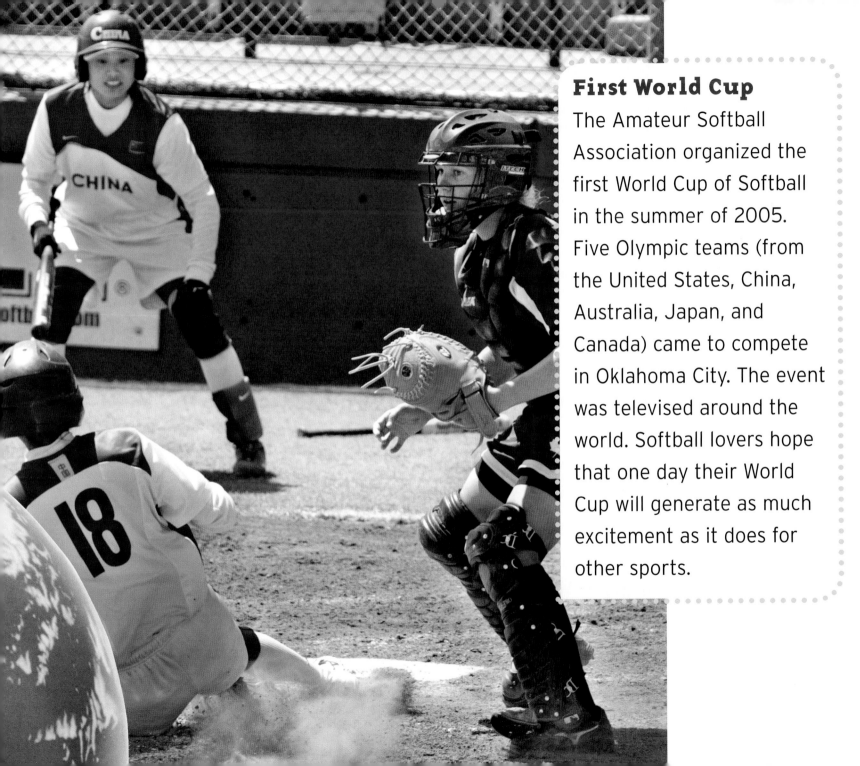

First World Cup

The Amateur Softball Association organized the first World Cup of Softball in the summer of 2005. Five Olympic teams (from the United States, China, Australia, Japan, and Canada) came to compete in Oklahoma City. The event was televised around the world. Softball lovers hope that one day their World Cup will generate as much excitement as it does for other sports.

Stars of the Diamond

The most well-known and accomplished softball players in the United States are women.

LISA FERNANDEZ

Lisa Fernandez is one of the best fast-pitch softball players in the world. Born in California on February 22, 1971, she began playing softball as a child. She quickly became the star of the St. Joseph High School team in Lakewood, California. Lisa went on to play at the University of California, Los Angeles (UCLA), where she won a national championship and broke national and school records. She graduated in 1995 and joined the coaching staff of UCLA's team. As a pitcher and third baseman, Fernandez won three Olympic gold medals, three Pan American Games gold medals, and numerous other prestigious awards.

CRYSTL BUSTOS

Third baseman and home-run hitter Crystl Bustos was born September 8, 1977, in Florida. She attended junior college in Palm Beach, Florida, and was twice named the junior college player of the year. Bustos has won three Olympic gold medals and the same number of Pan American Games golds. She's played professional softball and has been ranked in the top five offensive players in the league. In the Olympics in Athens, Greece, Bustos broke the records for most home runs in the tournament and most runs batted in (RBIs). Bustos is continuing to gain recognition as a professional softball player for the Akron Racers in Ohio.

Going for the Gold!

Softball players and fans worldwide experienced great excitement in 1991. After 30 years of effort on the part of softball enthusiasts, the International Olympic Committee finally voted to add softball to the list of Olympic sports for women. Olympic softball was played for the first time in Atlanta, Georgia, in 1996. It was a huge success, attracting more than 120,000 spectators. The United States team won the first-ever gold medal in softball. The American women repeated their victory in the summer of 2000 in Sydney, Australia, and then again in 2004 in Athens, Greece. The victorious team became heroines for American girls, who began to recognize names like those of pitcher Lisa Fernandez and home-run hitter Crystl Bustos.

Sad Day for Softball

Unfortunately for Olympic softball hopefuls and fans everywhere, in 2005 the Olympic Committee decided to remove softball from the Olympics. Though it will be played at the 2008 games, by 2012 it will be no more. This will not be the end of softball's Olympic story, though. Softball associations around the world will continue to fight for its place on the program.

What Happened When?

1880 1890 1900 1910 1920 1930

1887 "Indoor baseball" is invented in Chicago.

1889 The first indoor baseball league is formed, calling itself the Mid Winter Indoor Baseball League of Chicago.

1895 Fire department lieutenant Louis Rober of Minneapolis adopts the game for his squadron, and it becomes known as Kitten Ball.

1925 Minneapolis Park Board changes the game's name to Diamond Ball.

1926 Walter Hakanson, of Denver's YMCA, suggests the name "softball" to the International Joint Rules Committee. The name sticks!

1933 Sporting goods salesmen Leo Ischer and Michael Pauley decide to organize softball on a national basis and invite 55 teams to play in conjunction with the 1933 World's Fair in Chicago.

1933 The Amateur Softball Association is founded to oversee softball play nationwide.

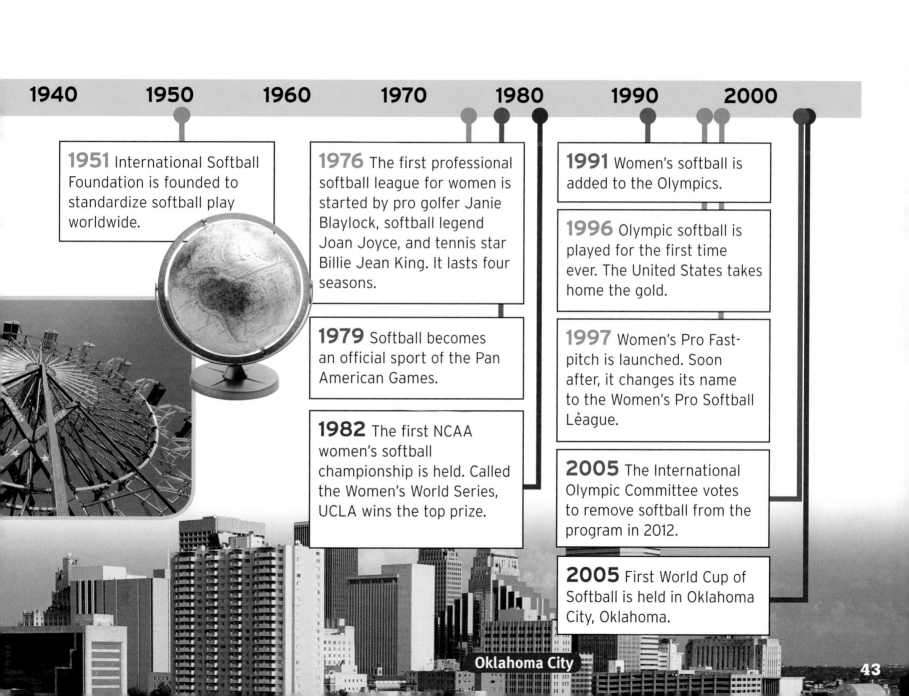

1940   1950   1960   1970   1980   1990   2000

1951 International Softball Foundation is founded to standardize softball play worldwide.

1976 The first professional softball league for women is started by pro golfer Janie Blaylock, softball legend Joan Joyce, and tennis star Billie Jean King. It lasts four seasons.

1979 Softball becomes an official sport of the Pan American Games.

1982 The first NCAA women's softball championship is held. Called the Women's World Series, UCLA wins the top prize.

1991 Women's softball is added to the Olympics.

1996 Olympic softball is played for the first time ever. The United States takes home the gold.

1997 Women's Pro Fast-pitch is launched. Soon after, it changes its name to the Women's Pro Softball League.

2005 The International Olympic Committee votes to remove softball from the program in 2012.

2005 First World Cup of Softball is held in Oklahoma City, Oklahoma.

Oklahoma City

Fun Softball Facts

Softball isn't the only descendant of George Hancock's indoor baseball; mush ball is another. In mush ball, defensive players don't wear gloves, but instead have to catch the 16-inch (41-cm) ball with their bare hands!

Bunting and base stealing are only allowed in fast-pitch softball.

Softball is played in more than 85 countries.

Chicago

In one early version of softball, the first batter in an inning could run either clockwise or counterclockwise around the bases. The batters that followed had to run in the same direction for the rest of that inning.

The National Softball Hall of Fame opened in 1973 in Oklahoma City, Oklahoma. It has about 300 inductees in categories including players, coaches, umpires, and sponsors.

Tee-ball is the game that first introduces kids as young as 4 to the wonders of softball. Instead of hitting pitches, young batters hit the ball off of a rubber tee that stands on home plate.

Kids and Kubs, a softball team founded in 1930, toured the country playing softball in 1931. The players were all over 75 years old and played wearing suits!

Softball Words to Know

ball: a pitch that's not a strike or doesn't cross the plate between the knees and armpits of the batter.

base: any one of the four corners of the softball infield that a batter must touch before scoring a run

base hit: a batter hits a pitch into fair territory and makes it to first base

bat: hard wood or metal apparatus used to hit the ball

batter: player currently up to bat

bunt: to hit a pitched ball gently, holding the bat horizontally

catcher: offensive player stationed behind home plate

center field: section of the outfield behind second base

count: number of balls and strikes a batter has made

diamond: the name for the softball playing field

fly ball: a ball that has been hit by a batter into the air

glove: protective hand equipment softball fielders wear on one hand to catch the ball

infield: area of the diamond that falls between the bases and home plate

inning: the dividing unit of softball in which each team has one turn at bat

left field: the area of the outfield between second and third base

line drive: a fly ball that moves without an arc, parallel to the ground

lineup: the batting order

mitt: equipment worn on the hand by the catcher and first baseman

out: term used to describe a runner who has been tagged by a fielder with the ball, or a batter whose fly ball has been caught

outfield: the part of the field behind and outside of the baselines

pitcher: the player who delivers the ball over the plate for batters to hit

pitching plate: the rubber apparatus the pitcher stands on

right field: area of the outfield between first and second base

roster: the list of players on the team

run: a point in softball, scored by a runner who reaches home plate after running all the bases

safe: term used to describe a runner who has made it to a base or home plate without getting tagged

steal: to advance to the next base before the ball has been put into play by the hitter

stick: to remain on base

strike: to swing and miss the ball or a pitch that arrives across the plate between the knees and armpits of the batter

tag: the move the fielder makes in touching either the base or the runner while holding the ball in his or her glove

tag off: a strategic move used by pitchers, in which they throw the ball at the base the runner is at, in between pitches, to catch the runner off guard and attempt to get them out

umpire: the official in charge of deciding whether runners are safe or out, pitches are balls or strikes, and hits are fair or foul

walk: to advance from home plate to first base without hitting the ball

Other Words to Know

accommodate: to adjust to the needs of another

arc: a curved line between two points

circumference: distance around the edge of a circle

collision: two or more moving people or things hitting each other

configuration: the way things are arranged and fit together

counterclockwise: moving in the opposite direction that the hands of a clock move

duration: the period of time that something lasts or exists

efficient: performing tasks in an organized way

informally: casually as opposed to ceremoniously

objective: something that one wants to achieve

retrieve: to bring something back

Where To Learn More

AT THE LIBRARY

Brockmeyer, Gretchen, and Diane Potter. *Softball: Steps to Success.* Champagne, Ill.: Human Kinetics Publishers, 1999.

Crisfield, Deborah, and John Monteleone. *The Louisville Slugger Complete Book of Women's Fast-Pitch Softball.* New York: Owl Books, 1999.

ON THE ROAD

National Softball Hall of Fame
2801 N.E. 50th Street
Oklahoma City, OK 73102
405/424-5266

Akron Racers Firestone Stadium
1575 Firestone Parkway
Akron, Ohio 44301
330/ 376-8188

ON THE WEB

For more information on this topic, use FactHound.

1. Go to *www.facthound.com*
2. Type in this book ID: 075651682X
3. Click on the *Fetch It* button.

FactHound will find the best Web sites for you.

INDEX

ABOUT THE AUTHOR

Darcy Lockman is a freelance writer and editor. Her work has appeared in the *New York Times*, *Rolling Stone* and *Seventeen*, among others. The author of several other nonfiction books for children, she lives in Brooklyn, New York, where she is currently at work on a series of mystery novels.